AF228610

BARBIE

RUTH HANDLER

Lee Slater

Big Buddy Books

An Imprint of Abdo Publishing
abdobooks.com

abdobooks.com

Published by Abdo Publishing, a division of ABDO, PO Box 398166, Minneapolis, Minnesota 55439.
Copyright © 2022 by Abdo Consulting Group, Inc. International copyrights reserved in all countries.
No part of this book may be reproduced in any form without written permission from the publisher.
Big Buddy Books™ is a trademark and logo of Abdo Publishing.

Printed in the United States of America, North Mankato, Minnesota
102021
012022

Design: Emily O'Malley, Mighty Media, Inc.
Production: Mighty Media, Inc.
Editor: Liz Salzmann
Cover Photographs: Anton_Ivanov/Shutterstock Images (car), Bettmann/Getty Images (Handler),
    DinosArt/Shutterstock Images (Barbie doll), Keith Homan/Shutterstock Images (lunch box),
    Walter Cicchetti/Shutterstock Images (Happy Meal)
Interior Photographs: AP Images, pp. 9, 28; Fiona Hanson - PA Images/Getty Images, p. 15; ivanastar/
    iStockphoto, pp. 17, 29 (bottom); JEAN-MARC BOUJU/AP Images, p. 27; Joe Haupt/Flickr, p. 11;
    logoboom/Shutterstock Images, p. 7; NeydtStock/Shutterstock Images, p. 21; ROBERT CLARK/
    AP Images, pp. 25, 29 (top); Ron Galella/Getty Images, p. 5; Science & Society Picture Library/
    Getty Images, p. 13; Sean P. Aune/Shutterstock Images, p. 19; Sueddeutsche Zeitung Photo/
    Alamy Photo, p. 23

Library of Congress Control Number: 2021942803

Publisher's Cataloging-in-Publication Data
Names: Slater, Lee, author.
Title: Barbie: Ruth Handler / by Lee Slater
Description: Minneapolis, Minnesota : Abdo Publishing, 2022 | Series: Toy stories | Includes online
    resources and index.
Identifiers: ISBN 9781532197079 (lib. bdg.) | ISBN 9781098219208 (ebook)
Subjects: LCSH: Handler, Ruth--Juvenile literature. | Barbie dolls--Juvenile literature. | Inventors--
    Juvenile literature. | Toys--Juvenile literature. | Mattel, Inc.--Juvenile literature.
Classification: DDC 338.47688--dc23

CONTENTS

RUTH HANDLER

Ruth Marianna Mosko was born on November 4, 1916, in Denver, Colorado. When she got married, she changed her name to Ruth Handler. She became known for inventing the Barbie doll. It is one of the most famous and popular dolls in the world!

Ruth Handler

MOVE TO HOLLYWOOD

In 1938, Ruth married Elliot Handler. They moved to Hollywood, California. In 1941, the Handlers had a daughter, Barbara. Around that time, they started a business making plastic products such as **jewelry** and candleholders. Their son, Kenneth, was born in 1944.

Ruth loved the glamour and style of Hollywood.
HOLLYWOOD

CHAPTER 3

MATTEL CREATIONS

In 1945, the Handlers started Mattel Creations with Elliot's friend Harold "Matt" Matson. The name was a combination of Matt and Elliot.

Matson left the company after a few years. The Handlers became the owners. By 1955, the business was very successful.

Ruth and Elliot Handler
at their Mattel office

CHAPTER 4

GROWN-UP DOLLS

In the 1950s, most dolls looked like babies. Handler realized that girls preferred dolls that looked older. Girls could use these dolls to imagine their own **futures**.

Handler wanted girls to have dolls that could wear adult fashions and **accessories**. She thought Mattel Creations could make dolls like this.

Many girls in the 1950s played with paper dolls that looked like teenagers and adults.

CHAPTER 5

BARBIE'S INSPIRATION

In 1952, German **cartoonist** Reinhard Beuthien created the Lilli doll. In 1956, the Handlers took a trip to **Europe**. Ruth saw a Lilli doll there. It was just the kind of doll she wanted to make!

Handler brought a Lilli doll back to California. She had the team at Mattel work on creating a similar doll.

13

SUCCESS!

The first Barbie Teenage Fashion Model dolls came out in 1959. More than 350,000 sold in the first year. This made Barbie the best-selling doll of all time. Handler had given girls a whole new way to play, and they loved it!

The first Barbie doll wore a black-and-white swimsuit, sunglasses, and earrings.

CHAPTER 7

BARBIE MEETS KEN

Two years after Barbie's **debut**, Handler decided to give her a boyfriend. His name was Ken. He quickly became nearly as popular as Barbie. Over the years, Barbie and Ken's **outfits** changed to match the current fashions.

Barbie and Ken are named after the Handlers' children, Barbara and Kenneth.

CHAPTER 8

WORK & PLAY

Handler wanted Barbie to show girls that they could be anything they wanted. So, she started giving Barbie career choices.

Barbie has had many different jobs. These include doctor, firefighter, and astronaut. Today, Barbie has had more than 200 careers.

Barbie has even been an Olympic athlete!

CHAPTER 9

BARBIES & MORE

In 1967, Ruth Handler became president of Mattel. By then, Mattel made and sold many kinds of toys. It was the world's leading toy manufacturer.

It takes a team of more than 100 people to create a new Barbie. The entire process, from the idea to the store, takes between 3 and 18 months.

Each new look for Barbie includes accessories such as shoes and bags.

21

CHAPTER 10

BARBIE BUSINESS

Handler knew that without new **updates** and features, girls would soon become bored with Barbie. So, Handler invented friends for Barbie.

This did more than give Barbie companions. It also created business opportunities for Mattel. With more characters, the company could make and sell more toys.

Handler also oversaw the creation of Barbie's little sister, Skipper.

CHAPTER 11

LONG LIVES

The Handlers left Mattel in 1975. Barbie was an **international** success and the best-selling toy in world history. Ruth Handler lived to the age of 85. She died on April 27, 2002. Elliot Handler died on July 21, 2011. He was 95 years old.

Handler (*left*) with an actress dressed as Barbie at Barbie's thirty-fifth birthday party in 1994

HANDLER'S LEGACY

Barbie fulfilled Handler's dream of helping girls use their **imaginations** while playing. Barbie can be anything she wants to be. The children who play with her know they can have big dreams for their own **futures**.

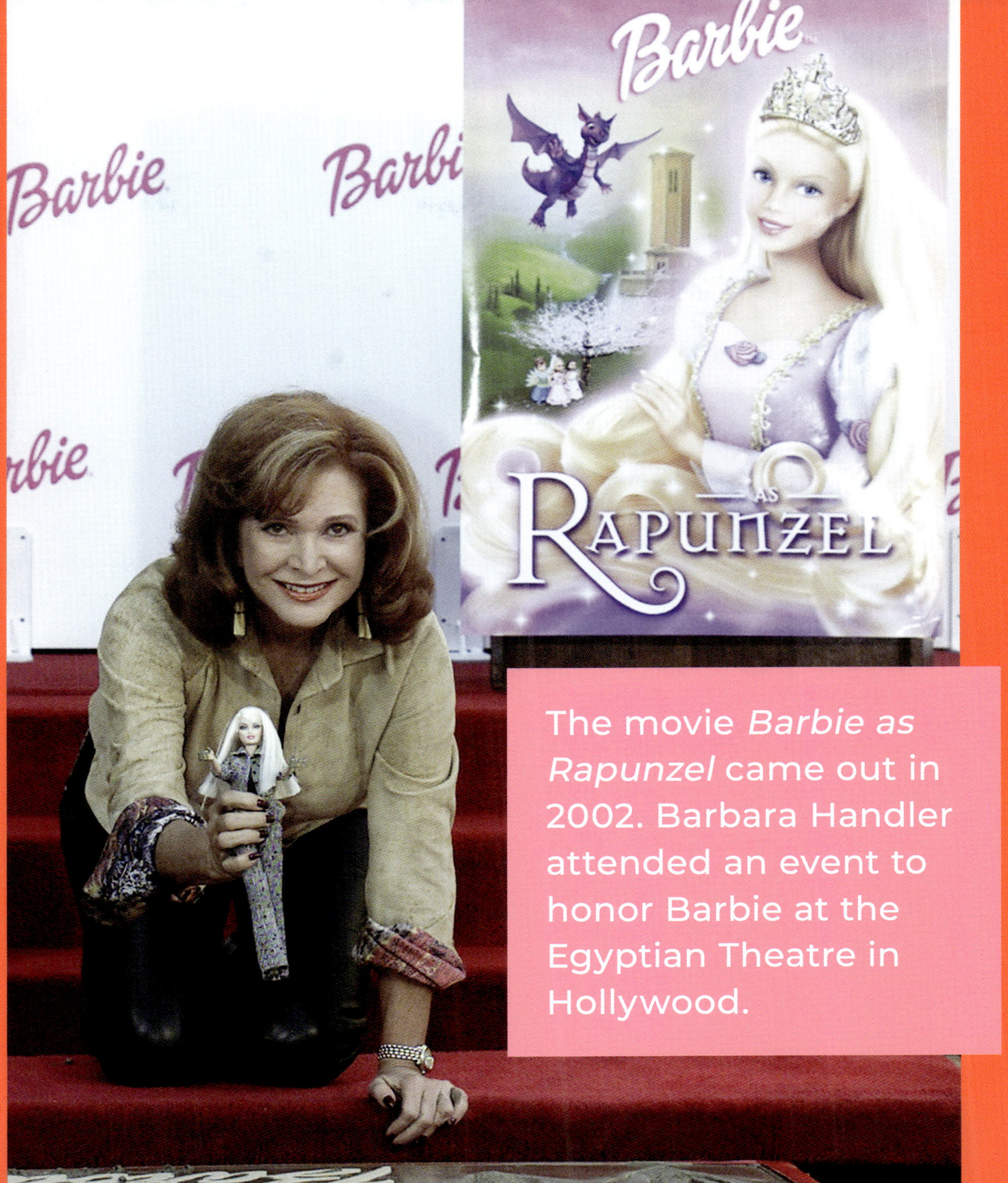

The movie *Barbie as Rapunzel* came out in 2002. Barbara Handler attended an event to honor Barbie at the Egyptian Theatre in Hollywood.

1916

Ruth Marianna Mosko is born in Denver, Colorado, on November 4.

1941

Daughter Barbara is born.

1945

Ruth and Elliot found Mattel Creations with Harold Matson.

1938

Ruth marries Elliot Handler.

1944

Son Kenneth is born.

1956

Handler finds the doll that inspires Barbie while visiting Europe.

1959

Mattel produces the first Barbie doll.

1967

Handler becomes president of Mattel.

1975

The Handlers leave Mattel.

2002

Ruth Handler dies on April 27.

accessory—something that is not necessary but makes something else more useful, attractive, or effective.

cartoonist—a person who makes drawings that are meant to be funny or tell a story.

debut (DAY-byoo)—a first appearance.

Europe—the continent between Asia and the Atlantic Ocean. England, Germany, and Italy are some of the countries in Europe.

future (FYOO-chuhr)—a time that has not yet occurred.

imagination—the creative ability to think up new ideas and form mental images of things that aren't real or present.

international (in-tuhr-NASH-nuhl)—of or relating to more than one nation.

jewelry—pretty things, such as rings and necklaces, that you wear for decoration.

outfit—articles of clothing worn together.

update—a more modern or up-to-date form of something.

ONLINE RESOURCES

To learn more about Barbie and Ruth Handler, please visit **abdobooklinks.com** or scan this QR code. These links are routinely monitored and updated to provide the most current information available.

INDEX